Look and Find

Illustrated by Animagination, Inc.

Written by Scott Wade

Published by
Louis Weber, C.E.O.
Publications International, Ltd.
7373 North Cicero Avenue
Lincolnwood, Illinois 60646

Manufactured in U.S.A.

8 7 6 5 4 3 2 1

ISBN 0-7853-1735-X

PUBLICATIONS INTERNATIONAL, LTD.

Welcome to The Puzzle Place, where there is always plenty of time for imagining, playing, reading books, and being friends. Can you put the pieces together and find all The Puzzle Place kids?

Skye

Julie

Kiki

Jody

Leon

Ben

The Piece Police

The Puzzle Place

WO MEN AT WORK

SHOW AND TELL

It's Show and Tell day at school. Some children have brought in pets and games, even little sisters and brothers. Each and every kid has something special to share—be it a special talent or a favorite game. There are many ways to share, and all of them are fun. But show and tell is probably number one. Can you find these Show and Tell items that The Puzzle Place kids are proud of?

Jody's new hat

Ben's pig, Hammy

Skye's necklace

Kiki's award-winning chili

Julie's Chinese dragon

Leon's solar system model

Mom

Dad

MY MOM

Scrub-a-dub-dub, put your pet in the tub! Bring your dog and your cat or other pet here. At the Pet Wash we clean even inside their ear. Some animals like water. Some animals don't. Find those that take baths and those who just won't. The Puzzle Place kids want their pets to get clean. They've brought them here today. Which ones have you seen?

Fish

Dog

Cat

Pig

Mouse

Horse

Perfume

Cat Walk

When you grow up, what do you want to be? A Career Fair has many jobs that you can go and see. Grown-ups who do different things will share their work with you. There are costumes and equipment that you can try out, too. The Puzzle Place kids have found careers that they have learned about. They're having fun at the Career Fair. Can you pick them out?

Firefighter Ben

Train driver Kiki

Dr. Julie

Painter Jody

Architect Skye

Magicians Sizzle and Nuzzle

Astronaut Leon

Cook Off

Make a Pizza

Puppeteer

Parades are special with lots of food and fun. Children watching, people marching, it's tons of fun for everyone. Join all The Puzzle Place kids as they have fun at the parade as it goes down Main Street. Try to find them all as they celebrate this special event.

Skye

Julie

Kiki

Jody

Ben

Leon

Costume Party

Hot diggety! There's a costume party in the basement. The Puzzle Place kids thought it would be fun to dress up in clothes they found in the basement, pretend to be famous people in history, and have a party! So come on down for fun and make history. Can you find The Puzzle Place kids dressed as these historical characters?

Pancho Villa

Julius Caesar

Alexander Graham Bell

Cleopatra

Abraham Lincoln

Amelia Earhart

3, 2, 1, blast off for fun! The kids from The Puzzle Place explore outer space. Join them to discover this wondrous place. Dressed up in space gear they're weightless and light, orbiting a world where stars light up the night. High up in space, far, far, from the ground, can you find The Puzzle Place kids floating around?

Sizzle

Nuzzle

Kiki

Julie

Leon

Jody

Skye

Ben

Musical instruments are like puzzle pieces, too. Each one is different just like me and you. Music from different cultures is what makes the world go round. So join The Puzzle Place Music Fest to find your favorite sound. Look for The Puzzle Place kids and Sizzle and Nuzzle enjoying the festival.

Skye

Leon

Jody and Kiki

Julie

Ben

Sizzle

Nuzzle

WORLD MUSIC FEST

WELCOME MUSIC LOVERS

Picture this! Pictures are a perfect way to share a memory. The Puzzle Place kids have photographs that they would like you to see. Sharing, caring, smiling, laughing times they have spent together. Pictures are a way to treasure them forever. Do you have a picture that you hold very dear? The Puzzle Place kids have picked some out. Can you find them here?

Leon's

Kiki's

Ben's

Jody's

Skye's

Julie's

Friends come in many shapes and sizes. Go back to The Puzzle Place and find these friendly surprises.

Sizzle
Nuzzle
A silly snake
A pink flamingo
A giraffe with a sweet tooth
A hungry hippo
A balloon baboon

Rub-a-dub-dub, lots of pets take a scrub. Now go back to the Pet Wash and find these animals playing in the tub.

Nuzzle
A monkey
A hippo
A zebra
A shark
An elephant

Let's go back to the school and take another look. See if you can find these Show and Tell things hidden in this book.

A goose with a golden egg
A soap box racer
A trampoline
A watercolor kit
A walkie-talkie
Tap shoes
A goldfish

Jobs, jobs, and more jobs. There are lots of things to try at the Career Fair. Can you find these people demonstrating their jobs?

Tree trimmer
Electrician
Sign painter
Trapeze artists
Guitar player
Writer
Puppeteer

March on back to the Parade to find all these things that make watching parades so much fun.

Toy soldier
Big tuba
Juggling clown
An upside-down walker
Stilt walker
Baton twirler
Tiny car